Gracie Finds Her Voice

BY JACOB WILLIAMS

ILLUSTRATED BY MARK SANDLIN

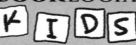
BOOKLOGIX
KIDS

Alpharetta, Georgia

Copyright © 2012, 2023 by Jacob Williams

Second Edition

ISBN: 978-1-61005-991-6 - Paperback
ISBN: 978-1-61005-992-3 - Hardcover

Library of Congress Control Number: 2023909168

Book design and illustration by Mark Sandlin
Photoshop production by Laura Nalesnik
Design production by Felicia Kahn

♾ This paper meets the requirements of ANSI/NISO Z39.48-1992 (Permanence of Paper)

0 5 2 5 2 3

I dedicate this book to my mom,
Angela Williams, and her organization
Angela's Voice.
My hope is that *Gracie Finds Her Voice*
will touch lives and save a child.

Foreword

As a prosecutor of child abuse and sex crimes in New York City with over fifteen years of experience, I have seen the horrors of child sexual abuse up close. I can tell you firsthand the devastation it leaves in its wake. Early on in my career, I discovered that most children do not immediately disclose when they are being sexually abused. As a result, the abuse often continues and escalates. Over the years, I have asked children why they did not tell right away. The answer that comes up repeatedly is simply: "He said it was our secret." It occurred to me that children needed to be taught that their bodies are private. They needed to hear that no one has the right to touch their private parts, and if someone touches them, to tell a parent or teacher right away. I was inspired to write a children's book called *My Body Belongs to Me* to teach three- to eight-year-olds these important lessons.

When it comes to child sexual abuse, secrecy is the most powerful weapon in a predator's arsenal. Children should be encouraged to tell their parents about things that happen to them that make them feel scared, sad, or uncomfortable. If children have an open line of communication, they will be more inclined to alert an adult to something nefarious before it becomes a problem. *Gracie Finds Her Voice* is a simple tale that teaches an important lesson about how keeping secrets can impact a child. In a playful way, children will learn that keeping secrets is not healthy. This book will empower youngsters with the knowledge that no one should put them in a position to have to keep a secret—especially someone they love. It is a great tool to begin a vital discussion that should continue as the child gets older.

I encourage families to institute a "no secrets" rule. The way to effectuate this rule is as follows: If someone, even a grandparent, were to say something to a child, such as "I'll get you an ice cream later, but it will be our secret," firmly but politely say, "We don't do secrets in our family." Then turn to the child and say, "Right? We don't do secrets. We can tell each other everything." Often families are in search of a word that conveys a similar meaning. I suggest the word "surprise" as it connotes something that is not being shared right now but will soon be shared.

Predators know how to get to our youngsters. They know what children want and how to secure their silence. It is time we arm our children with information that can keep them safe. *Gracie Finds Her Voice* is an important first step in that direction.

Jill Starishevsky
Prosecutor, Child Abuse/Sex Crimes, NYC
Author, *My Body Belongs to Me*

Little Gracie loved school
Every single, little bit.
She loved the playground most of all
And she loved to run around it.

But she hit her toe on a rock
    And fell and scraped her knee.
The teacher made her go inside
    And have the nurse take a see.

A bandage and a lollipop
Had her feeling better fast.
But when she started back outside,
She heard a noise from her class!

7

She took a peek through the door
And saw her friend Grant inside!
He took a toy from the teacher's desk.
"Don't do that!" she cried.

Grant turned around quick,
And he looked really mad.
He was Gracie's friend, after all,
So it made her really sad.

9

"Don't tell anyone, Gracie,"
Grant said, "or I will get in trouble!
This can be our little secret."
That idea made Gracie's tummy bubble.

They heard the whistle blow,
        The class was on their way!
    "Promise me, Gracie!"
"I promise," she heard herself say.

That night, Gracie could not eat.
She felt sick and knew she should tell.
But she promised she wouldn't
And knew Grant would yell!

When she went up to her room
And crawled into her bed,
Her mommy came in
And patted her on the head.

13

"What's wrong, Gracie?"
   Her mother asked with worry.
"You can tell me anything,
   And I'll help you in a hurry."

Gracie shook her little head
And bit her lip with fear.
"If you don't tell me what's going on,
I can't protect you, my dear."

15

Gracie opened up her mouth,
Her sweet little head fell.
"I saw a friend do something bad,
But I promised I would not tell."

"Secrets are never good,"
Her mother said, like she knew.
"They leave you feeling really bad,
And you get stuck in them, like glue."

"So come on, Gracie, you can tell me.
When you say it, you will feel better."
But Gracie could not say a word.
No, she could not say a letter.

"Okay, Gracie. Maybe later,"
Her mother sadly said.
She stood up, turned out the light,
And tucked Gracie into bed.

19

Gracie tossed and turned,
She just could not fall asleep.
But soon enough, she nodded off,
And her sleep was very deep.

20

"Hey there, Gracie!"
Said a friendly voice she did not know.
She sat up and yawned
And opened her eyes real slow.

A fuzzy, purple creature
Was sitting on the ground!
And giant colorful flowers
Were growing all around!

22

"This place is awesome!"
Said Gracie with a smile.
It was the best she had felt
In quite a long while.

"I know it is,"
Said the Fuzzy thing with a grin.
"And you can always come back,
If you do something for me again."

"You see now, Gracie,
I'm the secret you've been keeping.
I'm not so bad now, am I?
As long as you stop speaking."

His words were really sweet,
And he looked really nice,
But that last little part,
Turned Gracie's heart into ice.

26

"What do you mean stop speaking?"
She asked with a whimper.
The images around her started to shimmer.

"I do not like that idea,"
Gracie said with fear.
The flowers and colors
All disappeared.

Dark clouds rolled in,
And the light went away.
The magical place
All turned to gray.

"I tried to play nice,"
The creature said as he grew.
"Now I will try mean!"
Gracie did not know
What to do!

31

The little fuzzy thing
Grew ten feet tall!
His teeth got really sharp,
But that was not all!

32

His eyes went dark red,
And his fur turned all black.
He grew nasty claws.
He was a monster,
And that is a fact!

But Gracie stood tall.
No she did not run.
She had been scared all day
But now she was done!

The big furry monster
Took a big monster leap.
And right on top of Gracie,
He fell in a heap.

But from inside the darkness,
A big "NO!" she screamed.
And the monster flew back
A hundred feet it seemed!

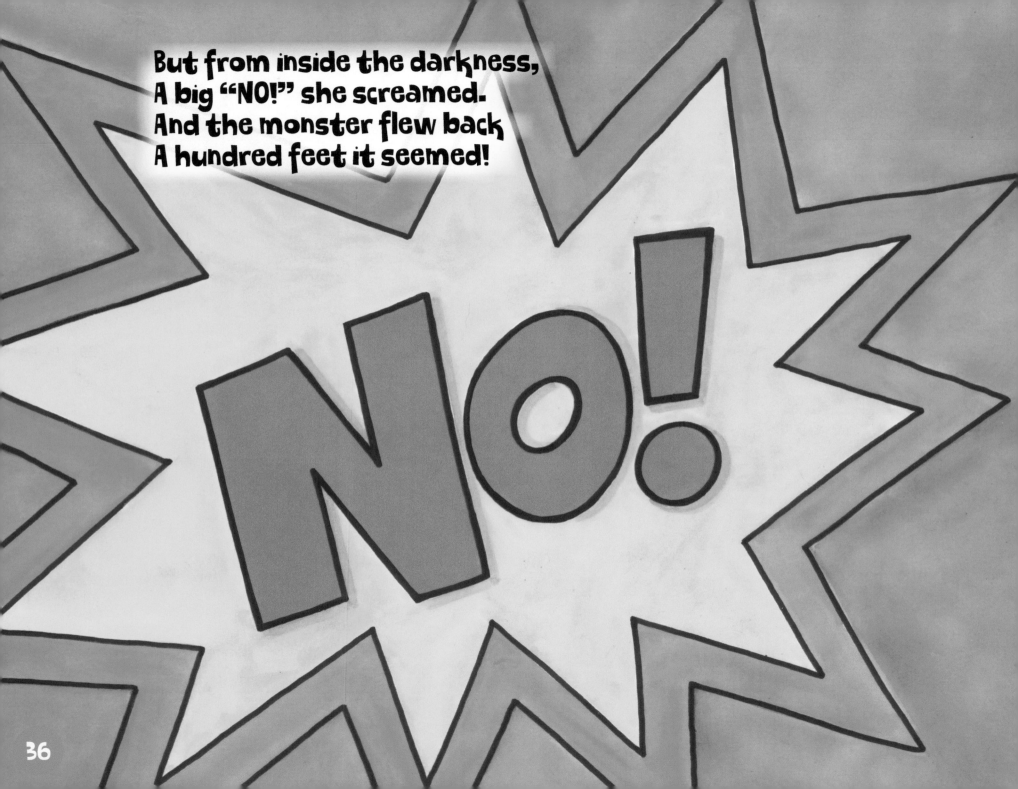

A new Gracie stood up,
All dressed for the fight.
She would never give up her voice,
Not when she knew what was right!

Her cape flew out behind her,
A big "V" glowed on her chest.
She brushed off her hands,
And she handled the rest.

"I will tell whoever I want!"
She yelled at the monster.
He shrunk down a size.
No, he could not beat her!

39

"I will tell my mom and dad,
    And they will always believe me!
I will tell my teacher or my friends,
    Even if it is not easy!"

"No matter what, I have my voice!
And you can never take it!
No, I'll use my weapon,
So be gone with you, secret!"

41

And all the whole time,
The monster did shrink.
And with the last line,
He went with a wink!

Poof! He was gone,
And the colors all returned!
Gracie could not wait to wake
And use what she learned!

43

Her alarm clock went off,
And she shot out of bed.
She went straight to her mom,
And the whole truth she said.

44

Gracie's mom called the teacher,
Who then called up Grant,
Who gave back the toy,
Then to school they both went.

"It's okay, Grant,"
Gracie said with a smile.
"Let me share what I learned!
And let's swing for a while."

Now use what you learned
From Gracie's adventure
To draw your secret you
Want to tell.

Angela's Voice

Angela's Voice is dedicated to developing, distributing, and endorsing valuable resources in the awareness, prevention, and healing of child sexual abuse. The materials, though specific for survivors of child sexual abuse, also benefit any abuse survivor and help protect children by teaching them how to defend themselves from abusive behavior. Founder Angela Williams, MFP, is a survivor-turned-advocate who shares a powerful message of triumph over tragedy by sharing her vulnerable and candid voice about her abuse trauma, her pain, her struggles, and her journey to healing in hopes that it may help other survivors expedite their healing journey.

 Williams has devoted years to providing awareness, prevention, and healing programs through her advocacy work. Williams has captivated audiences with her powerful message of triumph over tragedy as a victim of childhood physical and sexual abuse. At age seventeen, she attempted suicide, and that day was the end of her torment and the beginning of a journey to healing. She is a crusader for change and dedicates her life to eradicate child sexual abuse. She holds a master's in forensic psychology with a concentration in child abuse. Williams is a powerful messenger, appearing in national and international news and documentaries. She has been successful in state legislative reform and national policy work and served on the Policy Committee of the National Coalition to Prevent Child Sexual Abuse and Exploitation. She has received numerous accolades and awards for her work, including her collection of books that have valuable lessons for survivors of all ages.

Please follow Angela Williams on social media and contact angelasvoice.com
to book a speaking event or interview.

Books by Angela Williams

Loving Me: After Abuse

From Sorrows to Sapphires, Angela Williams's Memoir

Children's Books (Ages 5–10)

Gracie Finds Her Voice

Grant Gets His Shield

Gracie and Grant's Big Win

Gracie and Grant's Big Win Coloring Book

Find Your Voice Curriculum Book

Interactive Workbooks—Adults

Healing

Pathway to Healing, Guide to Healing

True Intimacy

Shattering the Shame

Unveiling Child Sexual Abuse

Prevention

Tough Talk to Tender Hearts

The Grooming Mystery

Single Parenting Solutions

Courage to Speak

Join the Angela's Voice Movement

HELP US SAVE THE NEXT GENERATION OF CHILDREN!

Take action to break the silence and cycle of Child Sexual Abuse and Exploitation

1 **Be a Child Advocate**

3 **Invite Angela Williams to Speak**

2 **Donate at angelasvoice.com**

4 **Purchase another Angela's Voice Prevention or Healing Book**

Discover more child sexual abuse prevention and healing resources at angelasvoice.com and follow angelasvoice on social media.

Instagram @Angelasvoice

Facebook @Angelasvoice

Twitter @Angelasvoice

Linkedin/angelasvoice

Angelasvoice.blogspot.com

Youtube.com/angelakwilliams